STRETCH

STRETCH

COMES HOME

a story about God's love

Written and Illustrated
by Justin Beaton

This book is dedicated to all of God's creation great and small.

A special thanks goes to Amy Beaton for proofreading and editing this book, to Kelli, Milani, and Amy for coming with to help adopt Stretch, and to Jeff for helping search for him.

Before he came to America, little Stretch lived in a faraway country called Qatar.

As a young kitten, he ran around on the streets because he had no home.

Each day, young Stretch did his best to survive, and all he ever wanted was to live with a loving family. Stretch didn't know it yet, but God was protecting him until he found them.

One day, a kitty rescue team from an animal shelter flew over to Stretch's country. Their mission was to rescue stray cats and bring them to America for loving families to adopt.

PET PASSPORT

R

ROYAL VET CLINIC

And guess what! Stretch was one of the kitties that was chosen!

Once he arrived in America, Stretch found himself at a strange but wonderful place called a cat café. He lived with many other rescued cats, and the nice people there took very good care of him.

Stretch was at the cat café for a long time. He was adopted once but brought back because the lady who adopted him couldn't keep him. Stretch was sad, but God knew that his permanent family would come very soon.

A man named Justin is visiting the cat café today. He always had cats when he was a kid, but he wants one of his own to love now that he is a grown-up.

SIP & PURR

Justin brings his mom, his wife, and his niece to visit, and they all like Stretch. Stretch walks right onto Justin's lap! Stretch knows this is going to be his new family. He is one happy kitty.

Stretch is so excited to be in his new home. He loves to run, jump, and play all day long. Amy especially loves his cute, pointy kitty ears.

Stretch loves living with Justin and Amy very much. He especially enjoys sitting in the window and watching the birds and squirrels play outside. This is a dream come true. He might even get some treats!

Justin takes Stretch in the backyard to run, jump, chase, and get some fresh air. He loves being outside!

Stretch is definitely the coolest cat on the block. He gets to go for rides in the car and go to the park in his kitty stroller. He loves going on outside adventures!

What a blessing that God protected him on his long journey to America and brought him safely to a loving family just like he always wanted.

Stretch wonders about exploring his new neighborhood, but it is too dangerous to let an indoor cat like Stretch go outside all by himself.

There are bigger wild animals, cars driving around, sharp objects, and things he could accidentally eat that could make him sick.

It is a very cold fall day, and Justin and Amy
are outside putting up Christmas decorations.
But something terrible has happened! Stretch got
a little too curious and snuck out the front door.

Oh no, this is not good at all! Stretch was born
in Qatar where it is really warm, so he's not used
to the cold Wisconsin weather.

Justin looked everywhere for Stretch, but he was nowhere to be found. Amy helped too, but she couldn't find him either. Justin's dad even came over and drove around the neighborhood to look for him.

It would be hard to find Stretch at night because it is so dark outside, so, they are praying that he won't get lost. They are all very sad.

Stretch probably just wanted to play and explore, but it is a new area to him, so Justin and Amy are worried.

HELP US FIND

STRETCH

They call both of their families, and everyone prays for God to bring Stretch home. God has protected Stretch his whole life, and they are asking Him to protect him once more.

Justin and Amy put Stretch's picture on the internet hoping someone will find him. Justin searches the neighborhood with a flashlight because cats have eyes that glow in the dark. They are worried because they don't know where he could be, but they trust God. God knows where Stretch is and will care for him...

...just like he always has.

Justin and Amy leave food on the porch for Stretch hoping he will see it. They are prepared to sleep on the couch in the living room every night so they can hear him if he comes back. They are waiting and waiting.

But then Amy has an idea!

She remembers that cats have a very strong
sense of smell. They gather things that have
familiar scents so Stretch can smell them
and find his way home.

One of the best things they leave outside is
his favorite blanket. They hope and pray
that God will use it to lead him back.

Oh, what a marvelous idea Amy has!

As Justin is setting more of Stretch's things on the front porch, he thinks he sees something. Was it a tail? Yes! Justin saw an orange tail run past the front porch! Could it be? Did Stretch smell the scent of his favorite blanket and find his way home?

It is Stretch!

He found his way home after being gone for six whole hours! When Amy opens the door, he looks cold, scared, and hesitant to come inside, but the warmth of his home is too good to pass up. He comes inside, and Justin and Amy are so glad!

They hug and hold Stretch for what seems like forever. He is so cold that he lays by the heating vents for hours.

Stretch is thankful to be home, and Justin and Amy are so joyful that he is okay! They tell their families the good news, and everyone is relieved.

Stretch sleeps through the night safe and sound in his nice warm kitty bed with his favorite blanket nearby.

Justin and Amy stay close to Stretch all night. They know their family would have been incomplete without him.

They are very grateful to God for bringing Stretch home. God protected him tonight just as he has for his entire life.

God guided him to his loving family—which was all Stretch ever wanted.

The story of Stretch's life and how God loves and protects him every day is a good reminder to us all.

It shows us that God cares about the little things in our lives just as much as he cares about the big things!

It doesn't matter if it's a butterfly or a blue whale—God loves and protects all of His creation, big and small.

That means that if you're sick or sad, you just lost your favorite toy, or you didn't have a good day at school, God cares about everything because most of all, he loves and cares about YOU!

God sure loves Stretch a whole lot, but he loves YOU even more!

Meet the Author
Justin Beaton

Justin and his lovely wife, Amy, live in Wisconsin with the stretchiest feline that you ever did see. They are starting their family and can't wait to introduce their future kids to Stretch!

FROM THE AUTHOR'S DESK

Dear reader,

Thank you for taking the time to read about Stretch and the first of his many adventures! Adopting a furry friend and giving them a warm, loving home is always a good choice! If you're interested in that, I encourage you to find a cat café near you.

Above all else, please remember the words of John 3:16 - "For God so loved the world, that he gave His only Son, that whoever believes in Him should not perish but have eternal life." You can always talk to God in prayer. He always listens and always cares. God Bless you!

-Justin

STRETCH
COMES HOME

Credits

This book was designed in Canva in conjunction with Adobe Photoshop, Affinity Photo 2, and BeFunky. All visual assets are primarily from Justin Beaton (actual photos converted to illustrations) and Canva. Pages 4-6, and 16-21 (only the larger image on page 19), were generated with Recraft AI and then edited. All story text was originally written by Justin Beaton and edited by Amy Beaton.

A special thanks goes to Astrid at Genesiz Designs for the initial template inspiration as well as some very timely guidance.

Made in the USA
Middletown, DE
22 December 2024

68074742R00020